About the Fruit

M. Joseph Young

©2006 M. Joseph Young
ISBN: 978-0-6151-6379-6

About the Author

M. Joseph Young has been involved in various ministries through music, broadcasting, teaching, and the Internet since the early 1970's. Currently chaplain of the international and interdenominational Christian Gamers Guild and host of the radio and Internet show A Quick Word, *he brings to his work an understanding of Christianity not fettered by particular denominational bounds. His broad background includes degrees in Biblical Studies from Luther College of the Bible and Liberal Arts (an arm of Lutheran Bible Ministries) and Gordon College, and a doctorate from Widener University School of Law. He has authored several other published books, including the acclaimed* What Does God Expect? A Gospel-based Approach to Christian Conduct.

Some of the material in this book was previously taught as part of the ministry of the band Cardiac Output, *and published as* The Fruit of the Spirit *on the author's web site, ©1998. Other sources are credited in the text or the notes.*

Contents

Fruit 1
    The Maturation Factor 4
    The Nature Factor 5
    The Fertilizer Factor...7
    The Nourishment Factor 10
    The Propagation Factor 11
    The Grafting Factor.......................................13
    Unity of the Fruit 15
    Love 17
    Joy 20
    Peace 24
    Patience 26
    Kindness..30
    Goodness 31
    Faithfulness 32
    Gentleness 33
    Self-control..35

Against Such Things There Is No Law 40
    Galatia 41
    From Saul to Paul..46
    Judaizers..52
    Nullifying God's Grace 58
    Living By the Spirit 63

Appendix: The Jerusalem Council 67

About the Cover 73

Fruit

> *But the fruit of the Spirit is love, joy, peace, patience, kindness, goodness, faithfulness, gentleness, self-control. Against such things there is no law.*[1]

The Apostle Paul wrote these words in his letter to the churches in Galatia, a substantial part of what is now central and northern Turkey. There were at least four cities in that region at which he had established churches, known as Derbe, Lystra, Iconium, and Pisidian Antioch,[2] and this, one of his earliest extant letters, was sent to all of them. In each of Paul's letters we find a few choice verses that are the frequently-quoted favorites. This verse, Galatians 5:22, is a popular verse in this book and one of the most popular in the Bible. Paul here presents the notion of the fruit of the Spirit, and we latch onto that idea.

What, though, does it mean?

Most Christians are pretty sure they know what it means. After all, we have heard this expression all of our lives, some of us, and certainly for as long as we have been Christians. Surely we know what "fruit of the Spirit" means; we speak of it all the time. Yet when asked, few can explain it beyond repeating the expression itself. We do not understand it.

Worse, Paul gives us little or nothing on which to base our understanding. He is contrasting

---

[1] Galatians 5:22f, here quoted from the Updated New American Standard Bible from Zondervan, the translation used herein unless otherwise indicated.
[2] In Acts 13 and 14, discussed below.

this to "the deeds of the flesh" mentioned a mere three verses before it, but there is nothing in the passage, nor indeed in the entire epistle, about fruit, nor about trees or vines nor anything normally associated with fruit. The word pops up here, never to be explained. Expanding our search, we find that fruit is often mentioned in the New Testament, but never elsewhere do we find this specific expression, "the fruit of the Spirit."[3] It is a unique statement to which we have come to attach great importance primarily because we like it. It certainly is an important statement; however, we need to understand it.

Certainly Jesus used the word "fruit" to speak of what people did, but He used it in other ways as well, such as speaking of the effect of the gospel in the lives of people. Other New Testament writers also used the word. However, none of those books had yet been written at the time this epistle was sent, and it is unclear how much of what Jesus specifically taught is familiar in Galatia, hundreds of miles across the sea from Jerusalem, at a time when very few Christian missionaries have taught anything. Further, although they speak of the fruit of righteousness,[4] the fruit of light,[5] good fruit and evil fruit,[6] fruits of repentance,[7] the fruit of labor or

---

[3] The King James Version and a few other older translations give this reading at Ephesians 5:9. It is a good translation of a corrupted text. The overwhelming weight of textual evidence gives that passage as "the fruit of light". A few copyists in early centuries recalled this Galatians passage when they were copying the Ephesians passage and "corrected" the text they were copying to match their recollection.

[4] Philippians 1:11, Hebrews 12:11, James 3:18

[5] Ephesians 5:9, see note 3 above.

[6] Matthew 7:17, 7:18, 12:33, Luke 6:43

ministry,[8] and the fruit of our lips,[9] it is not clear that any of these are what Paul intends when he speaks of the fruit of the Spirit here. Paul somehow expected that the Galatians would understand something from his use of the word "fruit" solely by the context within which he used it.

It might be that he believes they have heard the expression before. That would mean that he used the expression himself when he preached to them. Although this is possible, it seems unlikely, particularly given that he never uses the expression again. If it was so very familiar a part of his preaching at that point in his ministry, why does it not appear in other early epistles, such as Thessalonians or Corinthians? If it was so central to his message, why does he not use the phrase in writing to Rome, when he seems so intent on expounding the core of his gospel message for them? He might have used the expression when he was in Galatia but later abandoned it, but then we must ask what was wrong with it that he found it less than useful as his ministry grew.[10] It seems rather that we must accept that at this moment, when he was writing this epistle, he saw this as the

---

[7] Matthew 3:8
[8] Philippians 1:22
[9] Hebrews 13:15
[10] This is particularly highlighted by the fact that this epistle was intended as a circular, to be carried to four churches. It is easy to understand how an expression such as "all things are lawful" might have been used by Paul in addressing the questions and concerns of a single group and then not used elsewhere, as appears to have happened with Corinth, and considerably more difficult to apply the same reasoning to preaching over several churches which would have had cultural differences, accompanied by different questions and problems.

right word to express an idea he wanted his readers to grasp. If so, though, we must understand why he used that word if we are to grasp that idea.

It turns out that there are several truths about fruit that Paul may well have intended for us to understand in this context. Before we give any consideration to what the fruit of the Spirit is, that is, what things Paul identifies with it, we need to understand what it is, in the sense of why it is called "fruit".

The Maturation Factor

It is often said that the best time to visit Washington, DC, is in the spring when the cherry trees are in bloom. After spending a winter with bare branches, these trees sprout the buds of leaves but also the tiny hardened forms that gradually open into beautifully colorful and fragrant flowers which we call blossoms. For a few weeks the streets are awash with the lovely subtle pink-white petals as the bees tickle them. Then it ends, the petals dropping to the ground and washing down drains or decaying to mulch, leaving behind hard lumps on the ends of stems which once supported blooms.

That is, more or less, how all fruit begins. A stem on a tree or vine sports a hardened bud which gradually softens then opens into the blossom. The blossom withers and drops away, leaving a hard lump that gradually grows and fills with water, sugars, and some sort of cellular pulp, all of which ripens gradually to the fullness we know as fruit. Whether it is a cherry or a watermelon, an apple or an orange, a pumpkin or a tomato, every fruit passes through the same stages of this process.

That means it takes time. No one expects to plant a watermelon seed in the back yard in the morning and harvest ripe watermelons in the afternoon. Few of us will eat apple blossoms, and even little green apples are not what we want. Fruit grows, and that growth process requires the full growing season for it to reach maturity.

In the same way, Paul is communicating to us that this thing called the fruit of the Spirit takes time to develop in our lives. We could call it the *maturation factor*. You can see it coming, first as a bud and a blossom and later as an unripe image of what it will be, but it is not fruit immediately and it is not good fruit for a long time. Even in its early form it is beautiful, but it is not finished. It long holds the hope of promise, but it takes time before it is ready.

Thus when Paul speaks of love, joy, peace, and the other things being in our lives, he is letting us know that they don't happen overnight. You are a Spirit Fruit Tree, and you are growing good Spirit Fruit, but it will not be finished for a long time yet to come, and you should not expect to be ready for harvest too quickly.

The Nature Factor

I heard a story from Stuart Briscoe which he maintains is absolutely true as an account of events from his own boyhood. It illustrates this aspect of fruit *growing* quite well, and also tells us something else about fruit that is important to our understanding.

When he and his brother were small boys, they would at times be sent to their room when they were bad. This was not a terribly effective punishment, however, as there was a large fruit tree right outside their window, and they would easily climb from the window to the branches of the fruit tree, down the trunk, over the back fence, and into the fields to play ball until they were tired, at which point they would come back over the fence, up the tree, through the window, and into bed without anyone knowing they had been gone.

One day they heard their father say to their mother, "Mary, this fruit tree hasn't borne fruit for years. Tomorrow morning I am going to cut it down."

They were horrified. This was their way of escape. They had to save the tree, but what could they do? They could not very easily go to their parents and say, please don't cut down the tree, because without it we'll be trapped in our room when you send us to bed early. Hope seemed pretty dim. However, they devised a plan. Going to bed early that night, they emptied their piggybanks and slipped out down the tree into town, where they bought all the apples they could find, and some black cotton. Then, returning home, they climbed into the tree and tied apples onto every branch they could reach, and went to bed waiting with bated breath for morning.

In the morning they heard their father go outside; then they heard him come right back inside. "Mary," he called, "you must come see this, it is the most remarkable thing I have ever seen. This fruit tree that hasn't borne fruit for years this morning is covered in apples. It is incredible, it is simply covered in big, red apples. I can't believe it! It's a pear tree."[11]

The point Stuart Briscoe makes is that you cannot tie fruit to the outside of a tree and have it look right, and it will never seem real if you are pretending you have the qualities of the fruit of the Spirit. Clarifying that, we must understand that the fruit on the outside is a reflection of the nature on the inside. Apple trees bear apples; pears grow on pear trees. The fruit that appears in your life springs from the nature of the life within you. You display the fruit of the Spirit because the Spirit is there. Thus we recognize within the word fruit what we might call the *nature factor*.

The Fertilizer Factor

We see, then, that fruit grows, and that it is an outward expression of the inner nature. There is another aspect of fruit that is significant, which I call the *fertilizer factor*. Fruit grows best in response to fertilizer. Understanding this can be a boon to understanding how to live the Christian life. There is going to be fertilizer, because that is what the fruit needs to prosper.

What is this fertilizer? In organic farming, growth is encouraged by burying the plant in manure. The manure provides the nutrients which the plant needs to produce the fruit. Thus if you

---

[11] For Stuart Briscoe's story, I must thank Reverend Jack Haberer, who recorded a number of teachings at the Jesus '73 festival for my edification years ago when we were both fresh out of high school. The Briscoe brothers succeeded, incidentally: the tree reportedly was spared.

expect to see growth of fruit in your life, you should correspondingly expect to be buried in manure.

Surely you have heard someone say, "Don't pray for patience unless you want trials." Indeed, Paul and James both point to trials as the path toward patience.[12] Patience, though, is on this list. It is something that grows from the Spirit within us. Thus we see that for patience to grow, it has to be put into situations which test it, buried in manure, as it were, so that it will be strengthened. Trials produce patience, because that is where we learn patience, as we endure the trials.

The same is true for each aspect of the fruit. It is easy to love those that are lovely, but if you pray that God would give you more love His answer will almost certainly be to put someone into your life who drives you absolutely bats. Joy is the ability to be happy in whatever circumstances you are, but if you never face trouble not only will you never develop joy, you won't even know whether you have it. Peace exists only amidst turmoil, and so turmoil is both the growth medium and the testing ground for it. We could go on all the way to self-control, which you only see when there is pressure on you to lose control. In every case, the growth of the fruit is dependent on those negative circumstances, the problems that afflict you, the fertilizer up to your neck which you really don't like but which is essential to your growth.

Thus if you pray for the fruit in your life, you will have a great deal of trouble.

---

[12] Paul in Romans 5:3, James in James 1:3. This is not intended as an exegesis of those passages, as the Greek word in both of those passages is different from that used here in Galatians.

Does this mean you should not pray for this? After all, doesn't God know how much trouble we should have? Sufficient unto the day is the trouble thereof, or something like that? Surely if praying for the fruit is going to bring trouble, we shouldn't pray for it.

The first answer to that is although we don't know how to pray as we ought, God does tell us what to pray. If God is telling you to pray for love, then the excuse that you don't want to deal with difficult people is nothing more than that, an excuse to disobey God. Do what God directs, and if that includes praying for patience, accept that there will be trials, and start praying.

The second answer, though, is that as Christians we should embrace growth and pursue maturity. Once we were younger, and thank God we have grown up. Few of us would really give up all we have learned to go back and go through it again. At the same time, none of us would prefer never to have learned those lessons, never to have gotten to our current understanding. The price of learning was worth the knowledge gained. In the same way, we must come to understand that passing through the trouble is worth the gain, that our maturity comes at a cost but a cost well worth paying. Just as many who have finished school realize the value of what they received, and quite a few even return to school willingly to learn more, so too the difficulties through which we have passed to reach this point, however harsh they were, have brought about something good in us, and if we have to pass through greater difficulties to see the growth of greater good, that should be something we desire, or at least accept willingly if not eagerly, on the road to being all that God intends us to be.

One more thing should be said on whether you should pray for fruit, in view of the fertilizer that is bound to come. It is irrelevant whether you pray for the fruit to mature or not. God does not need you to pray for these things. You already gave Him permission to bring this about in your life when you confessed Him as Lord. He has your consent. You signed a blank check, gave Him full authority to change whatever He wished, to make you a new creation. He might want you to pray for these things. It might be important for you to do so, so that you understand what is happening to you, why these problems are in your face, why you are buried in fertilizer. However, it is not that if you don't pray for these things your life will be easier. The fertilizer is coming, whether you want it or not. The fruit needs to grow, and the Gardener will see that it gets what it needs to do so. Expect it, embrace it when it arrives, and recognize that this is what causes the growth God has promised to bring about in your life.

<u>The Nourishment Factor</u>

All these things I saw long ago. I even wrote a web page describing these three aspects of fruit as Paul's intended meaning. Yet I missed what is perhaps the most important aspect of the idea of fruit. Eventually I realized it, and when people wrote to thank me for my page I wrote back giving them this fourth point.[13] Then, when I considered it again, I realized that there was yet another function

---

[13] Eventually someone wrote to me giving me the same thought, and I am grateful, although I had realized it by then and sent it to several people.

of fruit that might be important here, another answer to the same question I had failed to ask. That question is, why do trees produce fruit?

There is one sense in which they do it for us, so that we would have food. God has ordained that there be fruit in the world so that we can eat, survive, and grow strong. In this sense, the fruit is not for the tree at all, but for those who pick the fruit and feed on it.

In that sense, the fruit growing in your life is not actually for your benefit. It is for your benefit, in the sense that love and joy and peace will all make you feel better as you pass through the world; yet it is given to you to produce fruit so as to nourish others. It is not as much you as those around you that benefit from your kindness, your goodness, your gentleness. The fruit grows for them, and you have it so that you can give it to them, enriching their lives and helping them to grow as well. This, then, is the *nourishment factor*, that the fruit in your life is there for the benefit of others.

The Propagation Factor

The other point about fruit that I had missed which seemed so obvious once I saw it was also the answer to the question, why does the tree have fruit? It follows from the fact that the fruit is there for others to eat.

Fruit trees produce fruit, and animals take the fruit. Mostly they eat it immediately, but sometimes they carry it elsewhere to eat later. Humans have a tendency to eat the fruit and throw away the seeds, but that's not true for most animals; they eat the fruit, seeds and all, and the seeds, packed in their shells, pass through the digestive tracts and are scattered on the ground elsewhere.

Even when we dispose of the seeds, we often do so carelessly. I have over the last several years had watermelons growing in my back yard. It is not that we ever planted watermelons, but rather that when we serve it our sons spit the seeds out back there, along the back fence out of the way. As long as we don't mow them down, we often get watermelon plants springing up back there, eventually producing blossoms and even a couple of watermelons each year, from which seeds are scattered to continue the process. Often we also have pumpkins growing, because someone making a jack-o-lantern dropped seeds on the ground along the edge of the deck, and these will sprout and develop. These plants are growing far from their original sources, because we picked up the fruit and carried it elsewhere.

That, then, the *propagation factor*, is another reason Paul refers to this as fruit. The fruit carries the seed. You have peace in your life, and others see it and hunger for it. They take that peace from you, and are nourished by it, and with it the seed is planted in their life, and may produce fruit in them as well. Of course, as Jesus told us in the parable of the sower, not every seed will produce fruit. What matters is that some will. The fruit growing in your life will make people hungry, and as they seek to understand what it is that causes you to be as you are, they receive that seed, and the gospel is planted in their lives.

The Grafting Factor

There is yet one more aspect of fruit that matters in this context, one to which Jesus made reference when He spoke of the vine and the branches, an agricultural practice which was used in His time and still today. It raises a question about the interpretation of one of the critical words in this passage to which we all think we know the answer but which is not so easy to prove, and that is to whom or what is Paul referring by the word *Spirit*?

Most translations I have seen capitalize this word, taking the answer to the question for granted: we are speaking of God's Holy Spirit within us. This is not so self-evident a conclusion as might be assumed, though. Paul has not said it was the Holy Spirit. He has just contrasted it to the deeds of the flesh, which would point to part of ourselves. He might be discussing some conflict within us, between our good redeemed spirits and our wicked bodies. This, however, is not a Christian perspective on the nature of man. We are not, in Christian ideology, good spirits trapped in evil material bodies. Rather, we are creatures who were created good, spirit and body, who turned away from God, spirit and body. The wicked material world is a concept derived from the thoughts of Plato and common to gnosticism; it is not a Christian doctrine. Also, although Paul never uses the phrase "Holy Spirit" in this passage, he does use the word "Spirit" several times. While at no point would it be impossible to take it to refer to our own human spirit, it makes far more sense if understood as the Holy Spirit. We are twice instructed to walk by the Spirit, particularly if we live by the Spirit, and told that the Spirit and the flesh are set against each other. It seems the best understanding of this passage comes from taking Paul as referring to the Holy Spirit.

That being so, this is not the fruit of our own spirits, but the fruit of God's Spirit. That points us to the *grafting factor*.

It is very difficult to produce perfect apples, particularly when considering a specific variety such as Macintosh or Granny Smith or Delicious. Seeds are cross-pollinated, and so the seeds of a tree that produces particularly good apples might in turn produce a tree with mediocre apples. However, it takes years before a tree matures to the point that we could know what kind of apples it will produce. Thus when a tree produces good fruit, there is a way to multiply the productive capabilities of that one tree that is somewhat quicker and considerably more reliable than planting seeds. Apple seeds are planted, but as the saplings become strong enough to support limbs they are cut close to the ground, and a branch is trimmed off the good tree and inserted into the cut on the new tree. Because of the way trees grow, the sapling roots and the inserted branch support each other, and soon heal the scar so that the new tree is a new root supporting branches of the good tree from which the inserted branch was taken. The apples produced on that tree are not the apples that would have come from the seed that was planted here, from which the roots grew, but apples identical to those on the tree from which the branch was taken. That is, the fruit on this tree is really the fruit of the other tree.

That process is called grafting. We use it for many kinds of fruit, because when you find a tree that consistently produces better fruit you can increase the amount of good fruit from it as well as preventing the loss of this fruit by using other trees to bear it. Vineyards do this, and have been doing it since Jesus' day. This is the process He is describing in his allegory concerning the vine and the branches, a picture of being grafted into Him.

The picture is imperfect, as all analogies are. However, when Paul speaks of the fruit of the Spirit growing in our lives, he is presenting an image in which we are the trees but God's Spirit has been grafted into our lives so that instead of supporting our own branches and producing the fruit of our own selves, the Holy Spirit is our branches, our leaves, and the source of our fruit. The fruit of the Spirit of course springs from the Spirit, not from us. It appears in our lives to the degree that we have been replaced by Him.

Unity of the Fruit

The Greek word in this passage is in the singular, "fruit" not "fruits". Elsewhere scripture teaches about knowing people by their fruits, but here it is one fruit.[14] Paul is not speaking of nine different qualities that develop in your life. He is describing one quality using nine different words.

The distinction may be slight, but it is not insignificant. It would be inappropriate on one level to say that you have some of these fruits in your life but not others, because they are inherently inseparable. It is not that the fruits are love and

---

[14] This is admittedly weak exegetically. There are places in the New Testament where the Greek, like English, uses the singular corporately, as in "much fruit". Even so, there is a tendency for writers to use the plural to describe plurality of kind, while the singular may be used for plurality of number but of the same kind.

faithfulness, gentleness and self-control. It is rather that the one fruit that is growing in your life is all these things, in some measure, as it expresses itself in different ways in different contexts. That which is joy is also patience, that which is goodness is also peace. It is all the same fruit, one expression of the presence of God growing in your life which presents in different appearances according to the circumstances.

In human terms, it might be appropriate to say that one person exhibits much love but not much joy. What we need to understand, though, is that the expression of fruit in our lives is a total package, not nine different qualities that are growing separately but one quality that responds with a complexity that defies simple description. Love, joy, peace, patience, kindness, goodness, faithfulness, gentleness, and self-control are not names of nine kinds of fruit. These are descriptions of one object. In the same way that you might describe a man as tall, dark, and handsome, yet mean the same man, or a woman as sweet, gentle, and delicate, all being the same woman, so here we have nine words which describe what the fruit of the Spirit is, but it is all the one fruit. God is not growing apples, oranges, peaches, pears, and lemons on one tree. He is growing the one fruit that combines the qualities of apples, oranges, peaches, pears, and lemons.

We can of course discuss the nine aspects, the nine descriptors, used of the fruit; we must be mindful throughout, however, that there are not nine different things here, but one thing described nine different ways.

Love

      Over the past century in the Christian church more has been said and written about love than perhaps any other concept in the New Testament. Thanks to works such as C. S. Lewis' *The Four Loves* we have been made aware that there are different Greek words which correspond roughly to our idea of love, each with its own special meaning. Some have so confused the phrase in John's epistle that God is love[15] that we come to think the reverse, that love is God, and anything that appears to have as its motivation something we loosely label "love" must be a good and right thing.

      The outcome of this is that it is difficult to know what needs to be said about love. Some will no doubt have heard more about love than can be gained from the pages of the New Testament, more perhaps even than is true. Others will be surprised at the most basic and fundamental statements concerning it. Compounding this is the amount that the Bible says about love. Just the word used here, agape (ah-gah'-pay), appears in one hundred seven verses in the standard Greek text of the New Testament. Search almost any English translation for the word "love" and you will get considerably more. Many of those are fundamental in our understanding of our faith. Jesus said that the two most important commandments were to love God and to love our neighbors;[16] He also said that we

---

[15] I John 4:8 and I John 4:16
[16] Matthew 22:37ff. This is discussed in more depth in the author's previous book, *What Does God Expect? A Gospel-based Approach to Christian Conduct*.

should love our enemies,[17] and went so far as to say that the way others would know that we were His disciples was that we loved each other.[18] Paul wrote an entire chapter about love, I Corinthians 13, in which he not only described a quality of complete selflessness, he commended it as the means of organizing our fellowship in church, and concluded that love is greater than either faith or hope. John tells us in his epistles that love is the one commandment fundamental to our religion.[19] This is the tip of the iceberg, as it does not begin to address the passages which allude to love but never mention it. No one can doubt that the parable of the Prodigal Son[20] is about the love a father has for his son, yet the word "love" does not appear in most English translations nor does it contain one of the primary Greek words we translate "love". It says in one place that the father felt "compassion" for his son, and that is as close as it gets. Meanwhile, the Old Testament is filled with material about love in one form or another, from Song of Solomon's erotic image of marriage to Hosea's marriage to a prostitute to the psalmist's declarations of pure devotion. Entire volumes can be and have been written on this one word, without straying from its use in scripture. It might fairly be said that the Bible and the Christian faith are about love, and nothing that can be said about Christianity can be separated from love as a central theme.

      However, it does not always mean quite the same thing in every context. If we look at the two

---

[17] Matthew 5:44
[18] John 13:35
[19] e.g., I John 2:7ff, II John 5
[20] Luke 15:11ff

commandments, to love God and love your neighbor, it should appear that in that context love is something you do. To love your neighbor is to act toward him in a loving manner which treats him as important and attempts to serve his best interest. It is love in action. By contrast, the famous love passage in I Corinthians is describing an attitude, an aspect of who we are to be, the motivation from which actions spring. It is internal, finding outward expression in actions that are governed by this internal concern for others.

That is its meaning in this context. As a description of the fruit of the Spirit, this is the new nature within. It is an attitude, a motivation, a controller, a fundamental character trait of the spiritual man. He acts and reacts in ways that show love in his life.

Love might be defined as always wanting the best for the beloved. Here it is generalized; it does not specify who is the beloved. As such, it tells us that the fruit of the Spirit appears in the form of wanting the best for everyone. Thus the commandments, to love God, your neighbor, each other, and your enemies, are all actions flowing from this desire for everyone to receive the best. It is an attitude of service, because it motivates the lover to do whatever can be done for the beloved, who in this case is everyone.

Someone once asked me why, if we are saved solely by faith, Paul says love is greater than faith. The answer is simple. Faith is our ticket into all that God has for us, but all that God has for us, that into which we are entering, is love. It is the point of all God has done, and the work that the Holy Spirit is performing within us.

Joy

Joy is an inverse aspect of love. It is in some sense love's echo, love's feedback, love's response. It is more than that, but that is the main thing to notice about it here.

It might be possible to do an assessment of your own life, to consider how much of each aspect of the fruit has appeared, which are your strengths and which your weaknesses. I don't recommend it for a host of reasons. First, as soon as you identify something as a strength, it is entirely likely that you will land in circumstances that put it to the acid test. Second, if you are genuinely honest about yourself, such an assessment is bound to become depressing, as you will discover how little you have gained and how far you have to go. I only mention it because I considered doing it once, when I was thinking about writing this book. I would not dare to suggest that I found myself strong in any area, but I thought for certain that the area in which I was weakest was joy, and that if I was going to write this book I was going to have to come at least to a fuller understanding of that aspect of the fruit, hopefully also a fuller expression and experience of it in my life. That led me to see joy in a new light.

Good things are happening right now. They might not be happening to me; they might not be happening where I can see them. However, at any given moment in time, there are people in the world who can give you good reason for their happiness, because something good is happening. Maybe I know someone who has such a reason to be happy, and I know the reason; maybe I am not aware of knowing anyone in particular who has reason to be happy, but I know that someone is happy, and that someone has good reason to be happy.

How do I react to that? If indeed I have love that reaches everyone, should I not be glad for them, happy for their sakes? Do I have the capacity to find joy in the fact that someone, not me, has found success, or love, or confidence? Someone was saved today, and the angels are rejoicing in heaven. I don't know who it was, but can I not rejoice for them? If indeed I have that love for all, then the joys of anyone are my joys. I care about them, so it makes me happy that they are happy.

Those of us who are parents know this from experience. Some of us who are married, or who have been in close relationships, have seen it in our lives. Your love for your children means that when they are happy it resounds within you. My third son was a joy to have as a child, because he was always appreciative in an animated way of all his gifts. Granted that we gave some thought to what he might like, it was still wonderful to see him at his birthday or Christmas opening presents and exclaiming, "Just what I always wanted." Part of the joy was that we had succeeded in pleasing him, but more fundamentally it was that he was pleased, that he found pleasure in the gifts he had received. That this child we loved was so evidently happy gave us reason to be happy as well. Because we loved him, his joy was our joy.

Similarly, because we love all, any joy is our joy.

It is not always easy to find that joy. Sometimes someone else's joy is connected to our own pain, such as when a colleague is excited about getting the raise or promotion for which we had hoped, or a friend excitedly announces that he's marrying the girl we thought perfect for us, or the birth of a child in another family revives the sting of miscarriages or infant deaths or barrenness. Sometimes the disconnect is less direct, as when the best things happen to someone who has mistreated us or distanced themselves from us, and far from rejoicing with them we resent their happiness. On one level, these are our failure to love. We do not see how the happiness of another benefits us. Joy, as it springs from love, to some degree means that we will be happy about things that do not in any way benefit us. Yet in another sense, we can find the joy in the benefit that comes to us from the good fortune of others.

When good things happen to people, God is pleased. He likes to do good things for His creation, and He likes knowing that what He has done has made people happy. We are instructed to thank God,[21] to show our gratitude, and told that He inhabits the praises of His people.[22] Perhaps I cannot find any comfort in knowing that some good has happened to someone I don't know, or worse, someone who has brought pain to me. However, God rejoices at the good that happens to them, when it is truly good. He is made happy. Can I be happy because God, whom I love, is pleased at what has happened?

My wife often comes home from work with stories of the wonderful things God is doing in the lives of people with whom she works. I don't know these people. I couldn't pick them out of a police

---

[21] E.g., Colossians 3:17, I Thessalonians 5:18
[22] Psalm 22:3. The rendering "inhabits" is found in older translations, newer ones preferring renderings that suggest being enthroned or seated in the midst of those praises.

lineup. Often, because of patient confidentiality rules, she can't tell me who they are, or why this is a good thing. It is difficult for me to be joyful because of some good things I don't understand happening to some people I don't know. I have enough trouble relating to the good things that happen to people I do know. Yet it is evident that she is excited and happy about the things she has seen in their lives, and certainly I can be cheered by her happiness. If I realize that God is pleased with the good things that happen in the lives of my friends, total strangers, even my enemies, can I not be happy for that happiness? I can find joy in the joy that God has.

There is yet another step to this, though. If something good happened to someone, God did that. He gave them that opportunity to be happy. What God does in the world makes the world a better place. We are all connected, and whether we want to believe it or not the good things that happen to any one of us are good things for all of us, because the world is the better for it, and we are in the world. Thus if a couple has the joy of bearing a child in Somalia, or a Chinese family sees their daughter married, or a Norwegian writes a successful book, the world is a better place, and my life is better by some amount. Their joy is my joy, not merely because my love for them should make it mine, but because what is truly good for them is good for the world, and thus for me. God did something good in the world, and I should rejoice that the world is a better place, if not because of my love for everyone else who benefited, certainly because in some small way I benefited.

Joy lies in knowing that what God does is good, and so in seeing all the things about us as His wonders, His kindness, His love for us. We miss it because we are focused on those things which pull us down, but he charges us to set our minds on things above,[23] to think on the things that are good, true, and lovely,[24] to see the world as He sees it, as a place where good things are happening and there is reason to rejoice.

What, though, of the pain and trouble that comes into our lives? How can we be joyful in this? Remember with Joseph, that he said to his brothers, "You intended evil against me, but God intended it for good."[25] What happens in our lives is intended for good. Whether it is the fertilizer causing the fruit to grow or the proving time through which our light will shine to others, the adversity is something through which we can find joy. We should count it joy when we face trials, James tells us,[26] for this very reason, echoing the same thought from Paul[27] and similar words from Peter.[28] Joy comes from knowing that God is caring for us, and that whatever happens is in some way a good thing for us.

<u>Peace</u>

Not surprisingly, perhaps, this knowledge which springs up in our lives as joy also is the foundation for our peace. God is working all things together for good for those of us who love Him and

---

[23] Colossians 3:2
[24] Philippians 4:8
[25] Genesis 50:20
[26] James 1:2ff
[27] Romans 5:3ff
[28] I Peter 1:5ff

are called according to His purpose.[29] Why are we worried? Why are we distressed? God has everything in control.

In the Douglas Adams novel *The Hitchhiker's Guide to the Galaxy* the imagined book which is the subject of the title, a sort of tourist's information book for the entire universe, is said to have written on the cover in large letters the words "Don't Panic". The theory is that whatever happens, there will be something in this book that will help solve the problem. We ought to publish Bibles in that design. A good part of what God has said to us is, "Don't panic, I am in control."

A great deal of ink has been invested in books explaining the events of Revelation. I won't say that this has been wasted ink, as many have benefited from such expositions. However, the ones I have read seem generally to miss the critical point. Blessed is the one who reads this book and those who hear it read, it says,[30] without a word about understanding it. The message of the book of Revelation is this: God is on the throne. Throughout the book we see a world being ripped apart at the seams, against the background of God in heaven patiently working His plan for mankind. Nothing is outside His control, nothing has escaped His notice, nothing will foil His intentions. It may look like total chaos down here where we are, but it is all part of God's plan, it is all working together for our good and His glory, and it is all under control.

---

[29] Romans 8:28
[30] Revelation 1:3

What, then, is there to cause us worry? Relax, don't panic, be at peace. God knows what He's doing and He has not overlooked your needs.

Patience

Our understanding of what this thing, this fruit of the Spirit, is can take another step forward as we move from peace to patience. If I know that God has everything in control and there is no need to worry, I can wait for the outcome, because the outcome is going to be good, and nothing is going to happen that prevents God from caring for us.

It is interesting that the Greek word here is not the one commonly translated patience in many other passages of scripture. It could be understood as "long tempered" in the sense of being exactly the opposite of "short tempered", that it takes a great deal before you become angry or upset. Some of the older translations attempted to capture the distinction by rendering this word "longsuffering", a word which has unfortunately fallen into disuse in modern English. The concept of this word is that we have the ability to live with the problem for as long as it takes. Paul had what he called a thorn in his flesh,[31] and although it is never quite clear what that was, it does appear that he lived with it for the rest of his life. We understand that trouble, too, is a good thing, which is here for a good reason, which is helping to make us good people. If we have to suffer with it for an hour, a day, a week, or whether it will be with us for the rest of our lives, it's not a problem, because we will have this trouble for as

---

[31] II Corinthians 12:7

long as God knows we need it, and then He will take it away from us.

We also know that no problem lasts forever. Death is for us a step from the small, temporary troubled world to the vast glorious eternal presence of God. Paul looked forward to death, seeing his time on earth as a delay in reaching the reward of heaven necessitated by the needs of people around him to whom he was still to minister.[32] Our problems end when we take that final step that carries us out of this present evil age and into the age which is to come, the place prepared for us in the heavens by Christ Jesus. We know, ultimately, all of this is temporary. We will have no hunger that is not satisfied, no thirst that is not quenched, no need that is not met. There will be no disease or pain, no mortgages or bills, no lawyers or creditors, nothing but eternal fellowship with God and each other. We don't understand all that, but we know it is coming.

Is this pie in the sky by and by? Is this a religion that says we should buck up under our suffering because God will reward us once we're dead? It is not. Christianity is a faith that believes good things are happening in our lives right now. Yet even of Jesus it was said that for the joy set before Him He endured the cross, despising the shame.[33] There is something about knowing that the trouble that is on us now is not merely temporary but a mere moment in the passing of eternity and a pathway to the glorious future that makes the present suffering not merely endurable but embraceable, that this road, however difficult it

---

[32] Philippians 1:20ff
[33] Hebrews 12:2

may be to travel, is the road that leads home, and we will be home before we know it, and will look back on the journey as a short drive through the country where the problems we met were of no real consequence. Having that knowledge now, we can begin to see all that happens along the way from the perspective of having completed the journey.

    In my youth I went on many hikes and canoe trips with the Boy Scouts. Truth be told, these excursions were not particularly fun in themselves. Walking through mountain passes ten miles a day for a week was hard work, made the harder by the weight of all your food, clothing, bedding, shelter, and gear on your back. Slogging through shallows dragging a laden canoe over stony shoals was not much easier, and portaging around rapids and waterfalls, usually several miles through rough terrain and always while carrying not only all that you would have carried on a hike but also the boat itself on your shoulders, was a struggle. I remember on some of my first canoe trips stumbling along the path bearing only my pack and some piece of troop gear in my hands while older and stronger boys strode past me with heavy burdens. I remember, too, becoming one of those older and stronger boys, wearing a pack on my back, settling the weight of a canoe on my shoulders, and picking up a pair of water jugs with my hands, traveling five miles assisted by a younger boy to guide the front of the canoe along the way, then returning to do it again. It was hard work; at times it was grueling. No one could honestly have thought it fun to do it. Yet we did it not only willingly but eagerly, as we knew there was going to be a feeling of accomplishment in the end, that we were going to travel fifty, or a hundred, or two hundred miles, entirely by foot and paddle, and would look back to see what we had overcome. Knowing this, we found pleasure in the overcoming itself, as the burden lay heavy on our shoulders and our backs, as our feet ached, as our skin was burned in the sun, as we slept on hard ground in wet blankets under thin tarps which failed to resist pouring rains. There was joy in the journey not because it was a pleasant walk in the park but because we could see the present from the perspective of the future even as we were in the midst of it, and so knew that this was good. We could endure the hardships of the journey because we were confident in the knowledge that arriving would be a moment of exhilaration, and that anticipated joy infected the pain along the way.

      If it can be so for a simple canoe trip, it can be so for the journey through life. We are going to reach the end, and it will be glorious. We can easily suffer with the problems of the road, because we know where we're going and what a joy it will be to arrive. Not only can we endure, we can do so with gladness, borrowing the joy that lies ahead, seeing the present through the eyes of the inevitable future, understanding that one day we will look back at this as a great trip to the promised land, and we might as well see it that way now. If that's what it will be then, then that is what it is now, and it is a simple matter to endure something that in reality is the path to something grand. This is not pie in the sky by and by. It is joy right now because we can see the present as the great thing we will fully understand it to have been in the future.

Kindness

It is not easy to see this. When the world seems to be crumbling down around you, the sun darkened and the moon black, the rivers turned to blood, and the four horsemen apparently taking a particular interest in your personal circumstances, it is not easy to remember that God is on the throne and this, too, is completely within His dominion. When there are more bills than income and the wolf is at the door, it seems small comfort that God owns the cattle on a thousand hills and will never lack for resources. When the windows of heaven don't seem to open despite your own liberality and God seems less interested in your needs than you are in those of others around you, it is difficult to rejoice, to be at peace, or to be patient. Yet knowing that God loves us and will not harm us or allow us to come to harm, we can find joy in Him, peace in His care, and patience in His assurance that this is not more than we can bear.

We can also begin to understand that others, too, are suffering. Paul tells the Corinthians that the comfort we receive from Christ in the midst of our affliction enables us to comfort others in any affliction.[34] It is because we have found this assurance that God loves us and cares for us that we are able to spread this good news to others. It is because we have come to understand this loving care in the midst of our adversity that we are able to relate to those who are in the midst of adversity who cannot see that caring hand.

From this comes kindness. Some translations render it gentleness, but whichever

---

[34] II Corinthians 1:4

word you use it speaks of a practical goodness, a usefulness combined with moral excellence, an ability to help others solely for their sake. As Jesus suffered and so understands our suffering, so we too understand the suffering of others through what we suffer. Because we understand, we can minister gently, meeting the need without harming the patient.

Goodness

Where kindness speaks of practical goodness, the next word speaks of virtue and beneficence, an inherent goodness, good in and of itself.

When one of His questioners addressed him as "Good Teacher", Jesus challenged the phrase, stating that only God is good.[35] He was not arguing that it was incorrect to refer to Him as "good", but rather calling attention to the fact that to do so was to recognize God manifested through Him.

We are not good in the same sense that Jesus is, but we are good in much the same way: through the manifestation of God in our lives. As already mentioned, the fruit of the Spirit grows from God's Spirit in us, and so as it appears in our lives it is the revealing of God living within us and shining through us. As it was with Jesus, so with us people will say that we are good people, because they will see God when they look at us, to some initially small but hopefully ever growing degree. It is one thing to be the sort of person who is helpful in practical ways, gentle and kind; it is something more to be perceived as inherently good, the sort of

---

[35] Mark 10:17f; Luke 18:18f

person whom one could not imagine doing something maliciously or selfishly because he is just not that kind of person and could not possibly mean harm to anyone.

Faithfulness

The Greek word for "faith" has many of the same meanings as its English counterpart, but the nuances often escape our attention because of the fact that they are frequently represented by the single form of the word. Although we speak of "keeping faith" and "pledging faith", in the modern vernacular we usually express this idea as "fidelity" or "faithfulness". Thus where older translations rendered this "faith" more recent ones going back at least to the American Standard Version tend to prefer "faithfulness".

It is worth pausing to consider whether this is a correct rendering. After all, to say that faith is growing in your life, in the sense of your ability to trust God, is certainly consistent with the maturing Christian life as much as to say that faithfulness, in the sense of fidelity, is doing so. Given that the word here is most commonly translated "faith" and that "faith" has both meanings under consideration, on what grounds might translators decide that "faithfulness" is the correct rendering, eliminating the possibility that this might mean "trust"?

Although it perhaps cannot be said conclusively either way, "faithfulness" is more consistent within the context of descriptors. This is not nine things that the Spirit produces in our lives; this is one thing which is rich and deep and needs nine words to describe it. "Faith", in the sense of a growing trust in God, is intrinsically different from the other eight, being more an action, an attitude in a different sense, almost something you do. The others are much more inherently something you are, something you become. They are character traits where faith is decision. Also, these are to some degree less focused. Faith would almost certainly have as its object God, whereas these others are all in relation to other people. Fidelity is much more consistent with the others, describing the same thing with yet another aspect.

What, then, does fidelity describe, and how does this relate to goodness?

It is natural to think of faithfulness in terms of fidelity to God; yet neither the term nor the context require that. You can be faithful to your friends, your spouse, your word, or your character. It speaks both of a consistency and of a trustworthiness. To be faithful is to be one who can be trusted to do what you say, counted on to be there when needed, expected to be what you have been. It is a facet of integrity, the quality of consistent goodness. It is called reliability, in the sense that others can depend on you to do right by them. From practical kindness to beneficent goodness we now come to consistent faithfulness, the quality not merely of being good but of being good always.

Gentleness

Perhaps because Paul is describing several facets of one object he has used several words that are very close in meaning. Modern translations which used "kindness" previously tend to render this word "gentleness"; those which used "gentleness" previously prefer "meekness" here.

We could argue about what each of these words means in English, but the important question is what concept Paul was attempting to convey by the Greek word so rendered.

The root word behind this word means "mild"; it is the antithesis of "harsh", and so conveys the sort of gentleness that is not abrasive. We speak of a mild detergent in contrast to a harsh one, as a soap that won't irritate your skin or damage your clothes. We might think of sponges and scouring pads, some of which are labeled "less abrasive", designed so as not to scratch the surface being cleaned. These are images that may help us understand "gentleness".

The word appears only in the epistles in the New Testament, and quite frequently in connection with correcting others. In fact, Paul uses it himself a few verses later when he instructs that those who are spiritual should restore someone caught in any trespass "in a spirit of gentleness".[36] This should not be taken to suggest that gentleness necessarily involves correction; rather, the reverse is so, that correction necessarily requires gentleness.

With all this imagery in our minds, perhaps we can begin to comprehend what is intended by this penultimate descriptor.

Have you ever met anyone you could not help but dislike? There are those who just rub you the wrong way, who don't really do anything intentionally offensive yet seem to be offensive in everything they do. Conversely, there are people who are so sweet and gentle that it is difficult to dislike them. Much of that may be natural, that is, some people are just more socially adept than others

---

[36] Galatians 6:1

and some are less aggressive and more cooperative. Yet there is a gentleness in God's Spirit which is respectful, caring, thoughtful—none of these quite the right word for this, but all reflecting something of the idea.

This is not to say that the Spirit of God is not demanding, or that no one is ever uncomfortable in the presence of God. Nor does this mean that the gospel is not a stumbling block and an offense to some who would rather it were not true. It means only that God's Spirit is not abrasive, that it does not offend or irritate by its character. Those through whom God's Spirit is manifesting itself similarly will be people who are not abrasive, who do not make you feel uncomfortable simply because they are annoying.

All of this is to define a word by its negation, saying what it is not. What matters with gentleness is not what it is not, but what it is. As with the others it is a positive quality, something you have, something you exhibit, something you are. It is not exactly that you are not abrasive; it is that you are gentle. It is not that you are not harsh, but that you are gentle. It is not that you are inoffensive, but that you are gentle. God expresses Himself through the believer as gentleness.

Self-control

English lacks a single word for this last concept, and so most translations use the hyphenated "self-control" to express it. The Greek uses a compound word meaning something like "in strength", that is, strength inside, the ability to control yourself.

This reflects an interesting and difficult aspect of the entire Christian life. Jesus said, "I am the vine, you are the branches."[37] In the fifteenth chapter of John He speaks much about branches abiding in the vine, and so bearing fruit. Yet vines are not like trees; they really have no trunks. They have roots, but are mostly branches and branches off of branches. Thus the vine is the branches, and the branches are the vine. You can't really distinguish the one from the other. In the same way, you and Jesus have been fused into one being. In some sense, what you do, He does; what He does, you do—if you abide in Him and He in you. There is a unity of action here, an agreement.

In fantasy we sometimes encounter what are labeled *symbionts*. There are in the world many creatures living in symbiotic relationships, in which each creature gives and gains a benefit from the other, such as the microorganisms in your digestive tract which feed on what you eat and in the process enable you to absorb the nutrients, or the sea anemone and the anemonefish, the latter finding safety within the stinging tentacles of the former while luring prey and bringing food scraps to its host. Fantasy writers have taken this idea to another level and proposed the idea of two intelligent beings in a symbiotic relationship such that they were joined in one body. You'll find the idea in *Star Trek*, particularly in the character of Jadzia Dax in *Deep Space Nine*. It's a major concept in the science fiction television show *Stargate SG-1*, and predating that it was used in some popular Japanese animated films or anime. In this concept, because two creatures have been joined, the two minds have

---

[37] John 15:5

to find a way to agree concerning how to use the one body. When I was working on the fantasy game *Multiverser*[38] I had to consider ways in which this might work. There are really only four ways that it can happen.

One way that such a symbiosis between two intelligent beings could exist is that each of the minds has control over its part of the body, so that the person does one thing and the symbiont another and everyone hopes that we don't fall on our face because we've lost our balance, so we do our best to communicate with each other concerning what it is we're going to do. The second is that one of the two minds controls everything, and the other is its slave, so that whatever the one decides to do is what happens, the other just going along for the ride and hoping the one makes good decisions. The third way it can work is for both minds to have control of everything, but to have separate minds that must communicate with each other if they're going to work together; they can fight for control, interfere with each other, and get nothing done, or they can agree on what they wish to do. Finally, the two minds can be melded into one, in which their thoughts are in tune with each other and they collectively make decisions with little more

---

[38] The *Multiverser* game books and novels are available through the publisher Valdron Inc. It is a role playing game with a Christian cosmology, in which the players play characters in many different settings and genres. The work on symbionts included therein was done to provide support for the types of characters and creatures in settings such as those others mentioned. The author of this book is a primary contributing author of those materials, including rules, supplements, and fiction.

About the Fruit

dissonance in their choices than a normal person has trying to decide where to eat on an ordinary day.

Abiding in the vine is somewhat analogous to being in a kind of symbiotic relationship with Jesus. The ideal is to come into that melded mind, in which our thoughts and His thoughts are the same thoughts, in which we automatically do what He would do not because we think about what He would do but because we have come to think His thoughts ourselves, fused together with Him and doing quite unconsciously what He would do because it is exactly what we would do.

The obstacle is that we have the ability to control everything, to take over the body and do whatever we want to do. Jesus never does that, because that's not the relationship He wants with us and He has the self-control not to do it. We, however, do it all the time, wresting control of our lives and taking them in the directions we wish to go, whether for our own pleasure (nearly always for our own pleasure in some sense) or out of frustration with our inability to see where He is taking us or simply from fear that we are headed into trouble. We, our selves, will take over given the chance, and He will not fight us.

Inner strength is the ability to restrain yourself from doing that. Temptation may come to do something you know is wrong, but you know that Jesus would never do that, and that the power is right there for you not to do it if you will abide in Him. Fear may arise and push you in what you know is the wrong direction, but you know that Jesus is not afraid, that God is in control, and if you abide in Him you will not act from fear. By thinking in harmony with the Holy Spirit, you have the ability to stay in harmony with the Holy Spirit, and so not to allow your self to take you away from that. The fruit of the Spirit is also self-control, resting confident in the assurance that your self is going to stay in tune with God's self within you, and is not going to escape that unity with the Spirit. The Spirit produces within you the power to stay in tune with the Spirit.

Thus we see this one characteristic, the fruit of the Spirit, expressing itself in nine ways, as it springs from within us, expressing our new natures in response to the fertilizer, and nourishing others as it carries the seed into their lives, as we allow the Spirit to become the source of who we are. However, Paul has more to say on this subject which requires our attention and consideration.

Against Such Things There Is No Law

But the fruit of the Spirit is love, joy, peace, patience, kindness, goodness, faithfulness, gentleness, self-control. Against such things there is no law.[39]

We have looked at why Paul calls these qualities "fruit" and have unwrapped each word—love, joy, peace, patience, kindness, goodness, faithfulness, gentleness, and self-control—which he uses to describe that fruit. The last part of this verse, however, reminds us that it stands in the context of a letter, the Epistle to the Galatians, in which Paul is saying something more than just that you should let this fruit grow in your life. Although sometimes at the ends of his letters Paul will toss out a string of unrelated admonitions, he is not yet there. This verse is part of the greater concern of the book, and part of the answer to it. We must thus move beyond the verse to understanding the book itself if we are truly to understand why the verse is here and what it is communicating to us.

The final words of the verse are, "Against such things there is no law."[40] Law has been a critical concept throughout this book, and one which Paul has been opposing. It is easy to see that the fruit of the Spirit is contrasted against the deeds of the flesh in the verses immediately preceding these. It is harder to see how it relates to the Law.

---

[39] Galatians 5:22f, again from the Updated New American Standard Bible from Zondervan.
[40] Galatians 5:23b

In one sense, Paul here is saying it doesn't. It has nothing to do with the Law. In another sense, its presence here in what is the climax of the book suggests it must have everything to do with the Law, because this book is about the Christian's relationship with the Law.

To understand that relationship we must return to the beginning of the book; to understand the beginning of the book, however, we must recreate the backdrop against which it was written, the events that led up to this moment in the ministry of Paul and the lives of his readers. We need to extrapolate some information from these pages, but also to look at the history of the time, the Acts of the Apostles.

Galatia

It was on Paul's first missionary journey that he first visited southern Galatia.[41] He had left from Syrian Antioch, the church where he and Barnabas were recognized as ministers called to this work, and traveled by boat west and a bit south to the island Cyprus, preaching in two major cities there and then sailing north and a bit west to the port Perga in the coastal province of Pamphylia. Traveling north, they entered Galatia.

The Galatian province has an odd shape on the map, as its boundaries are marked by rivers and mountains. Part of its larger northern area borders on the Black Sea along the eastern quarter of its southern shore, and it extends west about three quarters of the length of that shore, although Bithynia and Pontus stand between it and the water

---

[41] These details are recorded in Acts 13 and 14.

for most of that length. At its western end it takes a southern turn between Cappadocia to the east and the Roman province they called Asia to the west, essentially taking the center of what we call Turkey. It does not reach the Mediterranean coast, but widens westward in this southern area, and so contains territory through which the land route from Europe to the Middle East passed. There were several cities along this well-traveled route, despite the fact that they were isolated from both the Mediterranean and the Black Seas, the former by mountains and the latter by distance.

Perga in Pamphylia is near the western edge of Galatia, and Paul left that city almost due north across the mountains into the section of Galatia known as Pisidia, and reached its largest city, Pisidian Antioch, that is, the city Antioch in the Pisidian region of the province Galatia, distinct from that other city Antioch in the province Syria in which Paul's home church was located. That can be confusing, but no more so than distinguishing Newark, New Jersey from Newark, Delaware. This is in the northwest corner of the small but populous southern part of Galatia, and something of a bottleneck for overland trade between two continents. Paul's team got there in Acts 13:14, and the rest of that chapter is devoted to their ministry and preaching there. The next chapter runs them east, through the cities of Iconium, Lystra, and Derbe, and then back west again through each of these to Pisidian Antioch, south to Perga, and by boat easterly directly back to Syria and home to the other Antioch by the end of chapter 14.

There is a lot of debate among modern scholars concerning exactly what order events took from there. We know that Paul and Barnabas "spent a long time with the disciples"[42] at Syrian Antioch. The next recorded trip they made was to Jerusalem, for the critical and pivotal Jerusalem Council in Acts 15.[43] After that, they returned to Syrian Antioch[44] where they continued to preach and teach in their home congregation,[45] and then, "after some days",[46] agreed to go on another missionary journey. This is where they disagreed over whether to take John Mark,[47] and so Barnabas took him and sailed back to Cyprus[48] and we know not where else, while Paul took Silas[49] on the overland root north through the province Cilicia,[50] passing through and probably stopping at his home town Tarsus which is on the main road through that province, and coming to Galatia this time from the east at Derbe.[51] From there they visited the other Galatian cities.[52]

    Acts does not tell us when Paul wrote the Galatian epistle; Luke ignores that aspect of Paul's ministry entirely, reporting his progress as he preached the gospel through the Roman Empire but glossing over the rest of his work. Indeed, "Acts of the Apostles" is a poorly-chosen name for the book, as it ignores the ministries of most of them, who we

---

[42] Acts 14:28
[43] Acts 15:2
[44] Acts 15:30
[45] Acts 15:35
[46] Acts 15:36
[47] Acts 15:37f
[48] Acts 15:39
[49] Acts 15:40
[50] Acts 15:41
[51] Acts 16:1
[52] Acts 16:1f. Pisidian Antioch is not named in these verses, but would be difficult to avoid on the western overland route described.

know from post-Biblical sources traveled and preached a great deal. We just saw an example of this narrow viewpoint in the statement that Barnabas went to Cyprus, without any further consideration of where he might have gone from there. This is because Luke is not really writing to tell us what the apostles did after Jesus ascended into heaven. He is writing to tell us how Jesus managed to carry His message from that small Jewish subculture in Jerusalem to reach the entire world, first by expanding from a Jewish denomination to an international faith, then by reaching the heart of the world, the seat of the Roman Empire, Rome. Luke's interests have nothing to do with what Paul did in his ministry, other than that Paul was the instrument by which the last leg of this was ultimately accomplished. That helps us understand a great deal about the Book of Acts in terms of why Luke recorded what he did, but it does not help us at all in placing this letter to the Galatian churches into the historic context.

    To complicate it, Paul does not tell us much in the letter that helps. He does not say where he was when he wrote it. Sometimes he will give the name of a scribe who actually put the words to paper for him while he dictated them, and we will be able to connect that scribe with a time or place in Paul's ministry, but in this case although one might infer that someone else penned most of it and he only scribed the last few verses himself,[53] we have

---

[53] In Galatians 6:11 he says, "See with what large letters I am writing to you with my own hand." It seems likely that he meant that at this point he had picked up the pen and was writing the rest himself, and thus that someone else had

no suggestion who that scribe might have been. Nor does he tell us who was to have carried the letter, another clue which sometimes helps to place a time and place on his works.

We do have a reference in the second chapter of the letter to a visit to Jerusalem, with Barnabas, after fourteen years.[54] Many think this is the Jerusalem Council of Acts 15; however, it is unlikely that this is so. Ultimately what Paul is describing in Galatians are the events which formed the gospel he preached on his first visit to the region, and the Jerusalem Council, falling after that visit, would be of no interest to that discussion. Further, it is difficult to find a reason why Paul would not have mentioned the decision of that council. He does appeal to his meeting in Jerusalem as giving support to the gospel he preached. There is no reason to think he would include their authority and not include the fact that they agreed and published their agreement to the church.

Thus we have a growing controversy within the church. Paul has been preaching a gospel to the gentiles which does not require them to be circumcised, and the Judaizers have been teaching his young converts that they really need to become fully Jewish if they wish to be fully Christian. He writes this letter to refute that position, and then as the letter travels west and north to Galatia, he

---

written the smaller letters that comprised the epistle prior to this point. However, it is possible that he meant that the entire epistle was written in large letters because he wrote it himself, so this is not conclusive. In any case, if someone else served as scribe for most of the letter Paul does not credit him.
[54] Galatians 2:1ff

travels south to Jerusalem to settle the matter for the whole church.[55]

From Saul to Paul

Who, then, were the Judaizers, and what was it that they taught which Paul found so objectionable? To get there, it may help to understand something about how Paul came to understand the gospel as he preached it. He tells us here[56] that his gospel was received by revelation, and it is interesting to imagine Paul sitting in Arabia for some unknown length of time[57] while Jesus dictated to him the message he was to preach. However, we know enough about who Paul was before He was a Christian, and enough about the one very specific revelation he received directly from Christ, that we can reconstruct the heart of his gospel entirely from those facts. In doing so, we can then discover what it was about the Judaizers that was wrong.

Saul of Tarsus was a Pharisee. The sect, or perhaps denomination, of the Pharisees was in some ways the closest to Christianity in many peripheral beliefs, and is the one sect from which modern Judaism traces its beliefs, although these have changed significantly over the centuries. The Protestant churches ultimately embraced the Old Testament canon which the Pharisees were at this time defining and studying. Other Jewish sects either denied that later books were scripture at all,

---

[55] For more on the place of the Jerusalem Council in this, see the Appendix: The Jerusalem Council.
[56] Galatians 2:2
[57] Galatians 1:17

or included intertestamental literature such as the Maccabean books, or didn't particularly think about scripture one way or the other. The Pharisees saw God's word in the Law, but also in what we would call the historical books, the poetic books, the books of wisdom—everything we embrace.

Studying those books, they made an observation from which they reached a conclusion. The observation was that God kept calling Israel to return to Him and keep the Law, and that when they did not do this He turned away from them and brought misery upon them. The conclusion was that those people who perfectly kept the Law would be so pleasing to God that He would bless them and send His Messiah to liberate them and lead them into the Kingdom of God on earth.[58]

Not only was Saul a Pharisee,[59] he was apparently a very serious and very good one. He came from a long line of Pharisees,[60] and studied with Rabban Gamaliel I,[61] whose words are still revered by the Jews today, preserved in the Talmud, the ultimate exposition of the Law. He dared later to say of himself that he had been blameless in terms of having kept the Law;[62] as near to the Pharisaic ideal of perfection as a man could be. He undoubtedly embraced the beliefs of the Pharisees, that God was going to send the redeeming Messiah

---

[58] Regrettably, I studied these Jewish sects so long ago I can no longer recall any of the sources for this, other than to cite my professor Dr. John Herzog of Gordon College, who taught an understanding of Paul's revelation of the gospel essentially the same as that presented here.
[59] Philippians 3:5
[60] Acts 23:6
[61] Acts 22:3
[62] Philippians 3:6

to them, to people like him who had dedicated their lives to understanding and keeping the Law of Moses in every particular.

The revelation that came did not have to say much to shatter this. By the ninth chapter of Acts Saul had recognized the danger of this new sect, a group who preached the absolutely impossible idea that the Messiah had come to sinners, not to righteous people; that the Christ had ignored and even disdained the efforts of so many good and sincere Pharisees to make themselves perfectly holy and had instead spent time with common working men and businessmen, government tax assessors, revolutionaries, and even prostitutes, and apparently had told them that the Kingdom of God was open to them. This had to be a false messiah, because the true Messiah had to come to the Pharisees. It was a fundamental doctrine in their faith, that they by being holy would earn the favor of God that brought the Messiah.

Yet here, on the road to Damascus, Paul confronts someone of such great power and majesty that he is compelled to call this person "Lord",[63] a title he would be loathe to use for anyone other than God. This august person then identifies Himself as Jesus,[64] and more than that He claims that Paul's attacks on these common sinners who constitute His followers are personal attacks against Him.[65] These people have not misrepresented Him or gotten the message wrong; they are teaching what He taught.

If Paul had no more revelation than that, it would be enough to provide his entire gospel, once

---

[63] Acts 9:5
[64] Acts 9:5
[65] Acts 9:4f

About the Fruit

he thought it through. It is proof that he is wrong, and that his teachers were all wrong, and his family all wrong. The most holy and righteous people in the world, the people most dedicated to being all that God wanted by keeping the law, by being good, were ignored and rejected by God in favor of sinners who didn't know more of the Law than they heard if they managed to make it to the synagogue on an occasional Sabbath morning instead of blatantly flaunting the Sabbath by carrying on business as usual.

If that is so, if the people who worked hardest to please God did not do it but these sinners were being embraced by God as His people, then it must be that keeping the Law has nothing to do with pleasing God. Paul had to go back to scripture to try to figure out what it was that he and every other Pharisee had missed, what it was that God really wanted that these people had that he did not.

The answer he found truly permeates the Old Testament. One only needs to see it. In Romans Paul points to Abraham[66] and to David[67] as examples of this, but we find examples all the way back to Abel[68] which Paul must have seen and

---

[66] Romans 4:1ff

[67] Romans 4:6ff

[68] Hebrews 11:4 tells us that Abel's sacrifice was accepted because of his faith. Looking at Genesis 4 to understand why the writer of Hebrews thought this, we see that Cain was a tiller of the soil, doing what God had commanded his father Adam that men should do, while Abel was trying to escape the effects of the curse by raising livestock and eating the meat (that he offered God the fat portions shows us that he was fully competent as a butcher, a skill you would not develop otherwise), which God did not allow men to do until after Noah. Thus here we already have the contrast between the one who comes to God based on Law being rejected and the

understood once he realized that the idea of pleasing God by keeping the rules was a mistake. That answer was that God accepts those who trust Him, who believe that God loves them and does not want to hurt them and is not going to lie to them or ill-use them or mistreat them, who rely on His mercy instead of on their own efforts.

    The author of Hebrews, in his roll call of those who had faith in Hebrews 11, points again and again to those who trusted God's word and God's mercy instead of their own goodness. Abel's sacrifice was one of a meat-eating butcher[69] who had completely ignored God's command that men should get their food by tilling the soil.[70] Enoch, who had no law, "walked with God", being pleasing to God not because he kept the rules but because he fellowshipped with his Creator.[71] Noah took God at His word when the Lord said there would be a flood, and spent a hundred years building a ship large enough for his family and all the animals.[72]

---

one who comes fully aware of his sin in hope of mercy being accepted.

[69] Genesis 4:4 states that Abel offered God "the fat portions", which demonstrates that he understood both how to butcher livestock and what parts of it had the best flavor. He was raising livestock for food, and eating the meat.

[70] In Genesis 3:18f Adam was commanded to eat "the plants of the field" raised or gathered by the "sweat of your face"; meat was not on the divinely approved menu until after the flood, in Genesis 9:3f.

[71] Genesis 5:19ff tells us most of what we know about Enoch. The writer of Hebrews tells us in 11:5 that "he obtained the witness that before his being taken up he was pleasing to God", which must be a reference to this statement that he "walked with God".

[72] According to Genesis 6:22, "Noah walked with God" also; in Genesis 6:22 he did what God told him in connection with

Abraham trusted what God told him many times, always acting on the basis of what God said, seeing the world through the eyes of faith, of that trust in God.[73] Joseph was so confident that God was going to return His people to their land that he left instructions to take his body back with them when it happened.[74] Against what must have seemed insurmountable obstacles, Moses believed that God was going to deliver His people from Egypt.[75] Joshua trusted that God was giving him Jericho, and followed the most absurd instructions concerning marching and blowing trumpets, knowing that if God said this was the way to do it, it was going to happen.[76] Even the woman Rahab of Jericho believed that if God said he was giving that city to Israel there was nothing that could stop it,[77] and for her reward she was not only spared the destruction that came on her people,[78] she became not only the

---

the Ark, trusting that if God said there was going to be a flood, it was going to happen.

[73] Hebrews 11 gives us his willingness to leave his home, the birth of his son Isaac (also credited to Sarah's faith), and his willingness to sacrifice Isaac at God's request.

[74] Genesis 50:25. Joseph was embalmed, mummified according to the customs of Egypt, and thus would not have decayed to the point that he could not make the journey. This was contrary to God's command of Genesis 3:19, "For you are dust, and to dust you shall return", demonstrating once again that it was not obedience to the law but trusting what God said that made men righteous in God's eyes.

[75] The author of Hebrews provide several examples of Moses' decisions to trust God, culminating in his trust that God would part the water for Israel to cross.

[76] Joshua 6 gives the full account. It begins with the city "tightly shut" and God's statement that He had already given it to Joshua.

[77] Joshua 2:9ff

[78] Joshua 6:25

great great grandmother of King David of Israel, but one of the great women in the lineage of Christ.[79] In long lists of great Old Testament figures, it is evident at every turn that what mattered was not doing the right thing but trusting what God said. That is what the Christians had realized that the Pharisees had not: you do not please God by being good enough, but simply by trusting Him.

That further meant that God would freely accept those who were not Jews, who were not circumcised, who were, in a word, gentiles, because keeping the Law didn't matter. It wasn't that it didn't matter if you slipped up a bit here and there; it was that there was no necessity to keeping the Law at all. If you didn't have to keep the Law, you didn't even have to be Jewish to be part of God's people. Thus you did not have to *become* Jewish to *become* one of God's people, and that meant you did not have to be circumcised, and you did not have to keep the Law, period, end of story.

Judaizers

However, there were those in the church who did not see this as Paul saw it. Paul was not the only Pharisee who had become Christian, but some of the others believed that you had to be Jewish to be Christian. After all, the Messiah was Jewish, and for quite some time all Christians were Jews, and in Jerusalem that was very much still the situation. Further, we have good reason to think that the Jewish Christians in Jerusalem, at least, were still keeping the details of the Law, some of

---

[79] This is summarized in Matthew 1, where her name appears in 1:5.

them more fully than they had ever done before.[80] Becoming Christian had not meant ceasing to be Jewish, in any sense of that word, and particularly in regard to observing the Law. There was no conflict between strict adherence to the law and faith in salvation through Christ. Would it not then follow that becoming Christian meant becoming Jewish, and so required adherence to that same Law?

    Circumcision was the starting point for this. It had been given to Abraham,[81] and Jacob's sons recognized that it was circumcision that defined them, and that was required of anyone who would become part of their family.[82] Even Moses was almost destroyed for having failed to circumcise his own sons.[83] If you were Jewish, you were circumcised to show that you were part of God's people, attached to God's covenant, and a follower of God's Law. Being circumcised made you Jewish. Being Jewish made you part of that covenant God made with Israel at Sinai. Being part of that covenant meant you were responsible to

---

[80] The Acts 15 Jerusalem Council would not have been held at all were the Christians ignoring the Law, as the entire question raised was whether gentile Christians had to obey the Law the way Jewish Christians were doing. Even Paul himself was still adhering very strictly to the Law of Moses, as evidenced by the fact that in Acts 21:23ff he agrees to undergo the purification rituals and present the sacrifices for a Nazirite vow specifically to prove that he had not abandoned the keeping of the Law nor preached to Jewish Christians that they should do so.
[81] Genesis 17:10
[82] Genesis 34:14ff
[83] Exodus 4:24ff

keep the Law that defined the terms of that covenant.[84]

Thus the Judaizers said that you had to have faith in Christ, but you also had to keep the Law of Moses. Exactly how they saw this relationship is not reported. Perhaps they thought that faith in Christ covered the failings all men had in trying to be sinlessly perfect, but did not absolve anyone of the obligation to attempt to do so as outlined in the Mosaic Law. Perhaps they thought that faith in Christ empowered one to keep that Law ever more surely, or motivated one to do so, or gave one the necessary understanding to see how it was to be done. Whatever the connection, they believed that all Christians either would or should desire to keep that Law in its perfect expression as delivered to Moses.

Paul disagreed. As we have seen, we can trace this disagreement back to the few details we know of his conversion experience, or we can assume that he had a much more detailed revelation at some point. However it was, Paul had a very different picture of the Christian's relationship to the Law, and he found the preaching of the Judaizers to be completely contrary to the gospel as he understood it.

Now look at how Paul contrasts the gospel against the law in Galatians. He draws the lines swiftly and surely, immediately asserting as he begins his letter that they have abandoned God and

---

[84] None of this has any bearing on the question of circumcision as a medical procedure. The debate over whether it is good medicine to circumcise boys is immaterial here. What matters is the religious significance of circumcision as a religious ritual inducting the individual into the people of Israel.

turned to a completely different and distorted message.[85] He declares that those who are preaching this distorted gospel ought to be cursed, and he writes it twice lest anyone think he is exaggerating.[86] He then gives the details of his preparation for ministry, including such contact as he had with the leaders of the Jerusalem church. Within that context, he observes that those leaders made no suggestion that Titus, a Greek believer, ought to be circumcised, and thus there was no reason for Paul to think that gentiles who came to faith in Christ had to be circumcised.[87]

He then characterizes his adversaries as "false brethren secretly brought in, who had sneaked in to spy out our liberty which we have in Christ Jesus, in order to bring us into bondage."[88] This is very strong language, almost as serious as his previous suggestion that they should be cursed. They aren't even really Christians, he says. They are spies, looking for ways to take our freedom from us.

Paul rightly ignored these people.[89] The church leadership, including particularly James, Peter, and John, was on his side,[90] and with their support and encouragement he was going to preach

---

[85] Galatians 1:6ff
[86] Galatians 1:8, 1:9
[87] Galatians 2:3. Again, Paul's reason for mentioning this here would seem to be that it fits into his preparations prior to that first missionary journey on which he preached his gospel to them. That he had brought Titus with him to Jerusalem and no one suggested the Greek believer be circumcised lends credibility to his assertion that the Jerusalem leadership were not advocates of circumcising gentile believers.
[88] Galatians 2:4
[89] Galatians 2:5
[90] Galatians 2:6ff

the gospel which he ultimately had preached to them.

In Galatians, though, Paul moves his tale forward to a moment when he alone stood for the principles of this gospel. In Jerusalem the church was so completely Jewish that no one ever had to think about how the gentiles fit into this. In Syrian Antioch, though, it was very different. Gentiles were a natural part of the church there, and Jews and gentiles within the church treated each other as equals. This does not mean that the Jewish believers ate pork, wore blended fabrics, or abandoned the Pesach celebration. It did mean that they treated their gentile brethren as brothers, fellowshipping with them, working together, and sharing meals. Paul and Barnabas were among the leaders of that church,[91] and that was how they did things. Peter came to visit, and fell right into the routine with everyone else.[92]

Suddenly it was all disrupted. Paul tells us that they were visited by some men from James.[93] He also says that Peter was afraid of what he calls the "party of the circumcision", and so he "held himself aloof". That is, he stopped sitting with the gentiles. Soon there was a "Jews only" table, and even Barnabas joined them.[94]

Paul then quotes his own words from that event, as he rebuked Peter specifically, and all the Jewish believers with him.[95] He accuses Peter of

---

[91] Acts 13:1
[92] Galatians 2:12
[93] Galatians 2:12. Note that he does not say that James took a different view, but that these men were somehow associated with him.
[94] Galatians 2:13
[95] Galatians 2:14ff

living like a gentile despite being a Jew—something which the Pharisee Saul would have understood keenly, that Israel was filled with people just like Peter who had never given the Law the kind of serious attention the Pharisees thought it deserved. He challenges Peter for suggesting through his actions that gentiles were in any way obliged to keep the Law that he himself had largely ignored all his life. Paul then includes himself, saying that those born Jewish could claim to be better than the gentiles, but in responding to the gospel of Christ he and they had set aside any idea that it was possible to be good enough to please God. "Knowing," he says, "that a man is not justified by the works of the Law but through faith in Christ Jesus, even we have believed in Christ Jesus, so that we may be justified by faith in Christ and not by the works of the Law; since by the works of the Law no flesh will be justified."[96]

      He hammers home this idea, that you cannot earn a not guilty sentence, you cannot be good enough to deserve commendation from God. The only thing you can do is forget about trying to be good and throw yourself on the mercy of God, believing that Jesus died so that you don't have to, that God is eager to accept us if we will just trust Him. It is not a matter of whether you are good enough for God. If you could be good enough for God, if you could earn your place in heaven, then Christ did not have to die. You cannot please God by keeping the Law. It cannot be done. You can only please God by trusting Him to save you. Any effort to be good enough for God nullifies God's grace.

---

[96] Galatians 2:16

Nullifying God's Grace

That idea of nullifying God's grace should cause us to draw back. After all, these people were not talking about doing terrible things. Paul is not worried about them committing indecent sexual acts, or worshipping idols, or slaughtering innocents. He is worried about them committing themselves to keep the Law, setting themselves to the task of being righteous individuals, living decent moral lives by following God's instructions. This is the horror at which Paul recoils, that the Galatians would decide to keep the Ten Commandments and the rest of it simply so that they would be good people.

He then begins contrasting a gospel based on faith against works of the Law. Did you receive the Spirit by earning it, or by trusting God for it?[97] Does God work miracles among you because of your works, or because you believe?[98] You became a Christian by trusting God; you started this life by letting the Spirit of God change you. If God started that work based on your faith, why do you think you have to finish it by your works? Having begun by the Spirit, he demands, are you now being perfected by the flesh?[99]

This should take us back to our discussion of the fruit of the Spirit. Paul is making it abundantly clear here that we don't find salvation by trying to do the right thing, and we don't grow in grace by trying to do the right thing. It starts with faith, it continues by faith, and in ends in faith. It is a work

---

[97] Galatians 3:2
[98] Galatians 3:5
[99] Galatians 3:3

of the Spirit of God within you that matters. It is not your effort to be good, or to do what the Bible says, or to live the Christian life. That is not merely irrelevant; it is counterproductive. Like being circumcised, focusing your attention on trying to do the right thing because you are trying to be good is exactly opposite of what God expects of us.

Before we reach that discussion, though, Paul needs to lay some groundwork. Between here and there, he presents some basic principles of the gospel. He covers much of this in Romans,[100] but here he hits all the key points. We are children of Abraham not because we keep the Law but because, like Abraham, we believe what God has said.[101] Even if we are descended from Abraham, it is clear from the Law itself that you cannot be justified by keeping the Law—you can only be justified by believing God, a fact to which the Law itself attests.[102] Since it is faith, not works, that makes you a child of Abraham, the gentiles become his children and heirs of the promise simply by trusting God.[103] His inheritance was based on the promise, not on the Law, and the Law cannot nullify the promise.[104] The Law was necessary to teach us our need for salvation.[105] However, once we have been saved, we no longer need the Law.[106] Hear that again: we no longer need the Law.

We come then to one of the most misunderstood verses in the entire Bible. It was for

---

[100] E.g., Romans 4
[101] Galatians 3:7
[102] Galatians 3:11
[103] Galatians 3:14
[104] Galatians 3:17
[105] Galatians 3:24
[106] Galatians 3:25

freedom that Christ set us free; therefore keep standing firm and do not be subject again to a yoke of slavery.[107] You may have been told that Paul is warning us against being slaves to sin, but he is not. You may have thought that he is admonishing us not to be slaves to our passions and desires, but that is not the case. Paul is telling us that we must not allow ourselves to become slaves of any effort to make ourselves righteous by keeping rules. We must stay clear of that kind of holiness, because that is works righteousness, the effort to prove to God that you deserve His blessing because you have earned it.

      Let's get it straight in our heads right now: you cannot *earn* God's blessing. You can never *deserve* God's blessing. You can never stand in the presence of God and tell Him that you're good enough that He should accept you, or that He must bless you because you did your part. You will never be good enough that you can stand in God's presence on your own merits; you can never earn anything by your efforts. The only basis on which anyone can stand in the presence of God is that God has offered to accept us as we are if we are willing to trust Him and believe that He will if He says so. To try to fix up our own lives under our own strength in accordance with some list of rules is to deny that God accepts us as we are. It is to spit on the grace of God, to trample the sacrifice of Christ. Stop trying to prove that you can be a good person, because that is not something you can be. As long as you believe that you have some hope of being good in your own strength, you are not relying on Christ or His Spirit.

---

[107] Galatians 5:1

Paul is so adamant about this that he makes one more very strong statement. He says that he wishes that those who were trying to persuade the Galatians to commit themselves to following the Law by being circumcised would take that knife and use it to end any possibility that they might ever be fathers of children who would continue the error.[108] There can be no doubt. The Christian life has nothing to do with keeping rules of any kind. That sort of thinking is Pharisaic, the belief that we will please God by our works. It has no place at all in the life of a Christian or the preaching of the gospel. You are not under Law but under grace,[109] and that means that trying to live the Christian life by following the rules is exactly the wrong way to do it.

The obvious question, then, is what is the right way to live the Christian life? If God does not give us the rules we are to follow, how are we supposed to become the kind of people He wants? It would be so easy if we could just make a list of the don'ts and follow that—don't smoke, don't drink, don't chew, don't go with girls who do. Paul appears to be saying to forget lists of rules entirely, because even if you could keep them perfectly that would not please God. By works of the law no flesh is justified. He drives that point home repeatedly. Yet if that is so, we are left with the burning unanswered question. What, then, does God want us to do?

Paul answers that question succinctly. The entire law is fulfilled in the single command, you

---

[108] Galatians 5:12
[109] Romans 6:14

About the Fruit

shall love your neighbor as yourself.[110] Forget the commandments. Forget the holy days, the rituals, the sacrifices, the restrictions, the obligations—you will never be able to do it all, and trying only makes it seem as if you believe you can. Just love people, and you will have done everything God wants you to do.[111]

You see, you were called to freedom[112]—a freedom that means you can and indeed should forget about all the rules and regulations, all the codes of conduct, all the right actions, all the "supposed to do" stuff you've ever heard. God is not interested in whether you live by the rules, no matter what rules you think He has given. He is interested in whether you trust Him, and if you do that is enough. However, now that you do not have to follow the rules, you have to figure out what you are going to do, and that is where you have the choice. You can turn your freedom into an opportunity for the flesh, which would be a bad choice, or you can serve others through love, which is what Paul recommends.

Paul speaks of the flesh, the desire of the flesh, and the deeds of the flesh. He contrasts these to the Spirit, walking by the Spirit, being led by the Spirit, living by the Spirit, and of course the fruit of the Spirit. The flesh and the Spirit oppose each other. If you walk by the Spirit, you will not fulfill the desire of the flesh. If you walk by the Spirit, you will bring forth the fruit of the Spirit in your

---

[110] Galatians 5:15
[111] The author has addressed this more fully in his previous book, *What Does God Expect? A Gospel-based Approach to Christian Conduct.*
[112] Galatians 5:14

life, and not be bound up in the deeds of the flesh.[113]

Further, it appears that you are not under law to the degree that you are led by the Spirit.[114] He has hammered home this idea that we are not under law, that we do not need to follow the law, that we should not listen to those who attempt to impose the law upon us, because we have been freed from the law and should not allow ourselves again to become slaves of the law. Walking by the Spirit frees us from the deeds of the flesh, and also from the curse of the law.

It thus would seem to be important for us to ask how to walk by the Spirit, how to live by the Spirit.

Living By the Spirit

For many people, those phrases conjure up something almost mystical. We have the idea that we would be in total harmony with God at all times, listening to Him, talking to Him, knowing His will in all things. We imagine that those who are truly spiritual, whatever that means, do this all the time, that they commune with God so completely that they can ask Him whether the potato salad needs more salt and hear His answer. That, we think, is walking by the Spirit, something to which we all aspire but most of us never attain. It is, we think, a sense of the presence of God which pervades us at all times. We probably don't know anyone who has come to that, but we figure there must be some out there somewhere.

---

[113] Galatians 5:13ff
[114] Galatians 5:18

I do not want to downplay the significance of a close relationship with God; nor do I want to suggest that this dream is impossible. Let me say that I share that dream, that hope that one day I will be so in tune with God that it will be quite normal for me to hear him say, "Stop at the Acme today, they have something on sale that you need."

Perhaps I trivialize this; yet perhaps it is precisely this aspect of God being interested in the minutia that appeals to us, that we would be in such complete and total fellowship with Him that the minutia would matter as much to Him as it does to us, and we would know His thoughts as surely as we know our own. We often desire that intimacy, that total relationship with our Creator.

That, we think, is walking by the Spirit.

It is not. I am confident that it is not. That experience, if it truly exists, is reserved for the few—Saint Bernard of Clairveaux, perhaps, or possibly Mother Theresa or Billy Graham—or for brief moments in our lives. It is not the experience of most Christians, nor even most pastors. If that is what Paul is asking, we can throw in the towel now. Not only is that beyond our experience, it takes this out of the realm of possibility. Those people who have that kind of relationship with God have been seeking Him for a very long time, and many others who have been seeking Him just as long, just as sincerely, just as devotedly, do not have that experience. It would mean that Paul was exhorting us to do what is not within our power to do, and making all the rewards of the Christian life contingent on our accomplishing it. Yet the Christian life is not about what we can accomplish. Becoming that intimate with God is not the means to the reward; it is the reward itself. It is not the path to right conduct, but the end result of seeking God.

Besides, Paul tells us right here how to walk by the Spirit. He does not say, "this is how you walk by the Spirit," but he makes it clear nonetheless. Several times he contrasts living by the Spirit with living by the flesh, but the first time he mentions the danger of following the flesh he gives a very clear and simple instruction as to how to avoid it: through love serve one another.[115] The contrast is between the Spirit and flesh, but it is also between loving service of each other and serving our own flesh.

I promised myself I would not dwell on the deeds of the flesh. We know that if we walk by the Spirit we will not fulfill the desires of the flesh, and these deeds will not appear in our lives. You should be able to see, though, that the simple choice lovingly to serve others will mean that it would be impossible for you to do any of these things—immorality, impurity, sensuality, idolatry, sorcery, enmities, strife, jealousy, outbursts of anger, disputes, dissensions, factions, envying, drunkenness, carousing, and things like these.[116] It would be impossible. You could not go there at all, if you were actively devoted to loving service of others. All you have to do to stay free of those deeds is to put others first, to serve one another in love. That is how you walk by the Spirit.

It also makes it clear how we get to the fruit of the Spirit.[117] If you are devoted to loving service of others, you will show them your love. You will

---

[115] Galatians 5:14
[116] Galatians 5:19ff
[117] Galatians 5:22f

rejoice in the good that happens to others, and know that all things that God brings to us are good. You will be at peace with those you serve, and with yourself, because you have nothing for which to fight. You can wait patiently, as a servant, and act with kindness, as one who loves. The acts of a loving servant are good, and the loving servant is faithful, and gentle, and self-controlled. Walk by the Spirit, not as some mystical experience but in a determined dedication to serve one another in love, and not only will you not do those things that are destructive to others and to yourself, you will become the kind of person whose life is rich with this fruit.

Appendix: The Jerusalem Council

The text jumps to the conclusion that Paul's reference to a meeting in Jerusalem is not to the Jerusalem Council of Acts 15. In the first draft of this book, this question was given a considerably more detailed examination. I agreed on consideration with my friend Dennis Coleman that this level of detail tended to derail the point of the book, and particularly if, as was in part intended, it was presented in lecture format. At the same time, the matter needed to be addressed, given the disagreement on the question. I don't presume that my conclusion (that Paul's Galatians reference is to his earlier meeting) will prove the final word on the matter, but I am confident of it myself, and so present the discussion and the arguments as I understand them.

First, although Paul mentions the time he spent in Syria and Cilicia presumably before his first missionary journey,[118] he does not mention having been to Galatia, Cyprus, or Pamphylia. Paul made a visit to Jerusalem between the time he began his ministry in Syrian Antioch and his departure for the trip to Galatia, recorded in Acts 11:30. Although few details are given in that verse, it is clear that Paul and Barnabas carried relief

---

[118] Galatians 1:21. We know that Paul was in Damascus in Syria from Acts 9:8 until Acts 9:26, when he made a visit to Jerusalem which accords with Galatians 1:18f, and from there was sent to Tarsus in Cilicia in Acts 9:30, where he remained until Acts 11:26 when Barnabas took him to help with the ministry at the church in Syrian Antioch. He appears to have remained there until beginning the first missionary journey in Acts 13:4. Thus the statement in Galatians fits the information in Acts to that point.

money to the elders at the Jerusalem church. That Luke does not mention any discussions at that time hardly tells us anything, as the duo certainly met with someone and said something. The details of the Jerusalem meeting Paul describes in Galatians 2 suggest a small, private meeting,[119] which quite fits the notion that Paul and Barnabas met with the elders to deliver the money and have a brief talk. Acts 15 is usually taken as being a considerably larger and more public meeting.[120] Also, Paul does not mention in Galatians that the Jerusalem Council decreed that circumcision was not for gentiles[121]—something which would have made most of the letter superfluous, if we believe that the authority of that council would have been recognized—but says only that they added nothing to his message but that the poor be remembered,[122] which is not recorded in the Acts 15 account, and overlooks the requests made by the Jerusalem church in terms of things gentile Christians ought to avoid so as not to offend Jewish Christians.[123] Remembering the poor, of course, is exactly what Paul and Barnabas were

---

[119] E.g., Paul says that he submitted his gospel "in private to those who were of reputation" in 2:2.
[120] See particularly 15:12, where "all the people kept silent" because they were listening to what Barnabas and Paul were reporting.
[121] Acts 15:18f
[122] Galatians 2:10
[123] Specifically in Acts 15:29 the Jerusalem church requested that gentiles abstain from things sacrificed to idols, blood, things that had been strangled, and fornication. None of these things are mentioned by Paul in connection with his meeting in Jerusalem, and the desire that they would remember the poor is absent from the Acts account.

doing in that earlier visit, as they were bringing aid to a church in the midst of famine.[124]

The one other detail that might be significant is that Paul says he took Titus with him to this meeting in Jerusalem.[125] Luke never mentions Titus anywhere in Acts, but does say that "some others" went with Paul and Barnabas to the Acts 15 meeting.[126] Unfortunately, the argument at this point becomes circular. On one side there are those who maintain that since Paul and Barnabas took Titus to their meeting in Jerusalem in Galatians 2, he must be one of those "others" mentioned in Acts 15, and since Titus was thus one of those others, this must be the meeting mentioned in Galatians 2. Opposing this is the observation that nothing in Acts 15 would compel us to believe that any uncircumcised Christian, let alone Titus specifically, was there, and thus the reference to taking him to Jerusalem in Galatians 2 must be referring to an earlier meeting Paul, Barnabas, and Titus had privately with Peter and James, and not to this larger event, because Titus does not appear to have been at the later meeting. That argument from silence does not work there or at the earlier meeting.

---

[124] Those who connect Paul's Galatians 2 visit with the Acts 15 council argue that the Acts 11 visit should be connected to his meeting with Peter in Galatians 1:18. Against this interpretation, the Acts 11 visit mentions Barnabas and a meeting with the elders, both of which are details reported in Galatians 2, whereas the Galatians 1 visit appears to have been Paul and Peter only, a detail of which he is pointedly clear, and thus would have to exclude Barnabas, James, and John. That Luke does not mention a yet earlier visit than the Acts 11 one is hardly telling, as he focuses on details that suit his purpose and ignores those which do not add to that.
[125] Galatians 2:1
[126] Acts 15:2

Although Luke mentions only Paul and Barnabas traveling to Jerusalem in Acts 11, he is generally disinterested in any effort to list traveling companions, particularly prior to the time he joined them during the yet to come second missionary journey, after which he had first hand knowledge of who was actually present when.

There is one point often overlooked in these discussions which I think critical. Paul is here describing to the Galatians where he got his gospel message, the message he preached when he came to them on his first missionary journey. What was decided by the Jerusalem Council subsequent to that journey would be irrelevant to the question of whether his message then was something given to him by God directly or something he got from the other apostles. He is defending his message based on that authority, that Jesus Himself gave him this gospel to preach. It makes no sense at all to bring up that yes, after he had visited them and preached in Galatia he went to Jerusalem, because this argument is entirely about what he preached in Galatia, a message that had been formed and delivered prior to the Jerusalem Council. Thus the Jerusalem Council is irrelevant to the question, and Paul's reference to a private meeting in Jerusalem must be to the one which occurred prior to the first missionary journey, quite a bit before the Jerusalem Council.

All of which is to say that we don't know when this was written in relation to that major moment in the church. It could be that Paul wrote this before, possibly even just before, heading to a meeting to fix this problem officially; it could possibly be that he came from that meeting and was back in Syrian Antioch preparing for whatever was to come. However, we do know that Paul has finished his first missionary journey. Further, it probably was not so long ago that he was there, as he speaks of them "so quickly deserting" the message he preached.[127] Whether or not the Jerusalem Council has been held, Paul is certain that the Galatians have slipped away from the central message of the gospel and turned to the legalistic practices of the sect we call the Judaizers, as evidenced by the suggestion that some were being circumcised.[128] It is most probable that Council has not been held, because it would have been so simple for Paul to have mentioned that the Jerusalem leaders have already agreed with him in rejecting the doctrine of the Judaizers, and saying so would not have compromised his authority nearly so much as some suggest,[129] and thus it is unlikely that he would overlook that meeting in this letter.

  I conclude, then, that Galatians was written from Syrian Antioch shortly after the conclusion of the First Missionary Journey, and some time prior to the Jerusalem Council. It would have been difficult for the Judaizers to appeal to the authority of James or others in Jerusalem subsequent to that

---

[127] Galatians 1:6

[128] Galatians 5:2. It may be that none had yet been circumcised, but the suggestion had been made that they should be, and they were confused on the issue.

[129] Paul references the combined opinion of the church in I Corinthians 11:16, where he makes the statement that the "churches of God" "have no practice" which differs from what he is telling them concerning the conduct of women in church, and his comment in Galatians 2:6 that "those who were of reputation contributed nothing to me" is already an appeal to the authority of the other apostles, stating that they do agree with his position even if they have never said so in any formal way.

meeting, given that a letter had been penned and sent from Jerusalem to which Paul could easily have referred in proving his case. The Epistle to the Galatians is a statement of the argument that led to that conclusion, written before the conclusion was widely promulgated, telling us exactly why gentile Christians need not be circumcised or keep the law even when Jewish Christians were doing so.

About the Cover

The images which grace the cover of this book predate, in concept, any thought of there being a book to accompany them.

In the early 1970s I was overhauling a guitar, and stripped it of its finish. I got an idea to decorate it with images of pieces of fruit, each one constructed of a word drawn from Galatians 5:22f, so that they would be the fruit of the Spirit. These I sketched and ultimately, with such meager artistic skills as I possessed, rendered as colored pencil drawings. Using decoupage, I affixed each of these to the face of the guitar.

A decade later, I lost that guitar. The images, however, remained I my mind, and when I was considering what to put on the front cover of this book they came back as a good idea that could be redone. I spoke with my son Tristan, who has most of the artistic talent in the family, and with some guidance and example from him, reproduced the images adequately, if not brilliantly.

Thought went into each selection, forging a connection between the idea of the word and the piece of fruit which represented it. At least some of that thought is worth sharing here.

The connection between love and apples is strong in stories, and it was very much this connection that inspired the idea for the entire set. Whether apples are connected with love because they are red and somewhat heart-shaped, or for some other reason, I could not guess; seeing that I could create the shape of an apple from the letters in the word "Love" made the entire idea come to life.

For joy, cherries were chosen. The three bursts of bright red have a fireworks-like appearance exploding on the page, a cheering and even exciting flash of light.

It happens that "peace" and "pear" begin with the same letters, and I suspect that influenced my choice. Pears, though, are soft in every way—soft to the teeth, a gentle yellow-green color, a light fragrance and flavor. Pear juice is often used in fruit blends, as it is never overpowering. They have a peaceful nature.

No fruit was ever considered for patience other than the lemon. The lemon is, after all, used metaphorically of anything for which patience is required, and the connection seemed too strong to ignore.

I am very fond of peaches, so their connection to kindness was natural for me. The sweet flavor, soft fruit, and particularly the warm and fuzzy exterior all fit the idea quite well.

Perhaps it is the combined efforts of the Florida and California orange growers, but of all fruits oranges seem the most wholesome. Loaded with vitamin C, known to fight colds and other illnesses, rich in juice and strong in flavor, and nearest to perfectly spherical of the familiar fruits, it seemed the natural choice for goodness.

There are many references in scripture to vineyards and grapevines and grapes, and quite a few of these are connected to faithfulness, to God's expectation that the fruit of His labor would be His, and not given to some other. Grapes also had the advantages that they were an unusual color that would provide contrast, and that it would be easy to put that many letters in a bunch.

There is nothing harsh about a banana, said one of my friends when I suggested it as a possible metaphoric image for gentleness, and that settled the matter.

I truly loved the idea of the watermelon to represent self-control. This largest of the familiar commonly eaten fruits grows on the ground, not swayed by wind, not moved by rain, not knocked loose from its connection to the vine. Few creatures can shift it or break it before it ripens and cracks open of its own accord. It sits immovable, the ideal image of firm resolve.

There were many delays in the process of producing this cover, and in retrospect perhaps any of the other ideas that were suggested along the way would have been quicker and easier, and might have resulted in a more appealing look for the book. However, I was eager to get the content to the many people who were requesting it, so when this was finally ready, I went to print.

About the Fruit

www.ingramcontent.com/pod-product-compliance
Lightning Source LLC
Chambersburg PA
CBHW020019050426
42450CB00005B/545